T0378879

Bear Grylls

HIKING ADVENTURES

Bear Grylls

This survival handbook has been specially put together to help young adventurers just like you to stay safe in the wild. Hiking is a fantastic way to get fit, and see some of the most incredible parts of the world, but it's vital that you are properly prepared to go out into the wild. Once you know what equipment to bring, and how to survive in extreme situations, then you're ready to go out into the wild and have some adventures!

Bear

CONTENTS

Let's go hiking!	4
Boots	13
Trailblazing	19
Jungle travel	21
Desert travel	23
Winter travel	29
Glacier hiking	34
Hill walking	39
Crossing rivers	41

LET'S GO HIKING!

Hiking is usually a long walk, often more vigorous than a gentle stroll. It is a great way to keep fit and explore the countryside. There are organized hiking groups available for people who want to join a club, or you can just plan your own route and enjoy being outdoors.

Backpacks

For anything longer than a short walk in the woods, you are going to need a comfortable backpack. The vast majority of backpacks sold today are the internal frame type, which offer excellent freedom of movement. They are typically built around two vertical aluminum staves and a rigid plastic sheet.

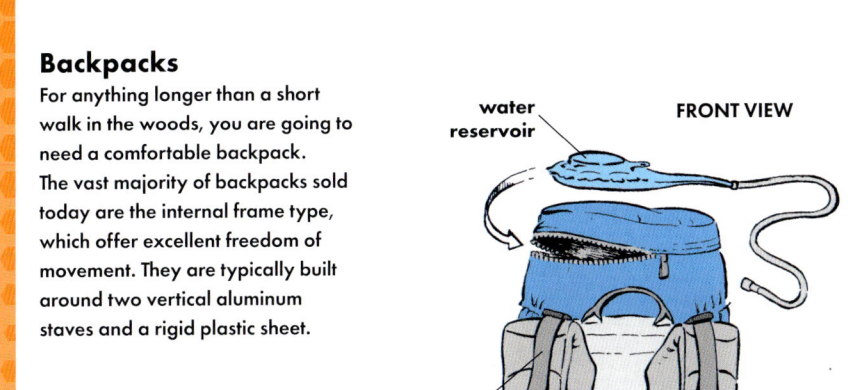

FRONT VIEW

water reservoir

shoulder harness

sternum strap

pocket

hip belt

side release buckle

BEAR SAYS

Test lots of different backpacks to find one that is comfortable since you will be carrying it for long distances. Load it up before you try it on.

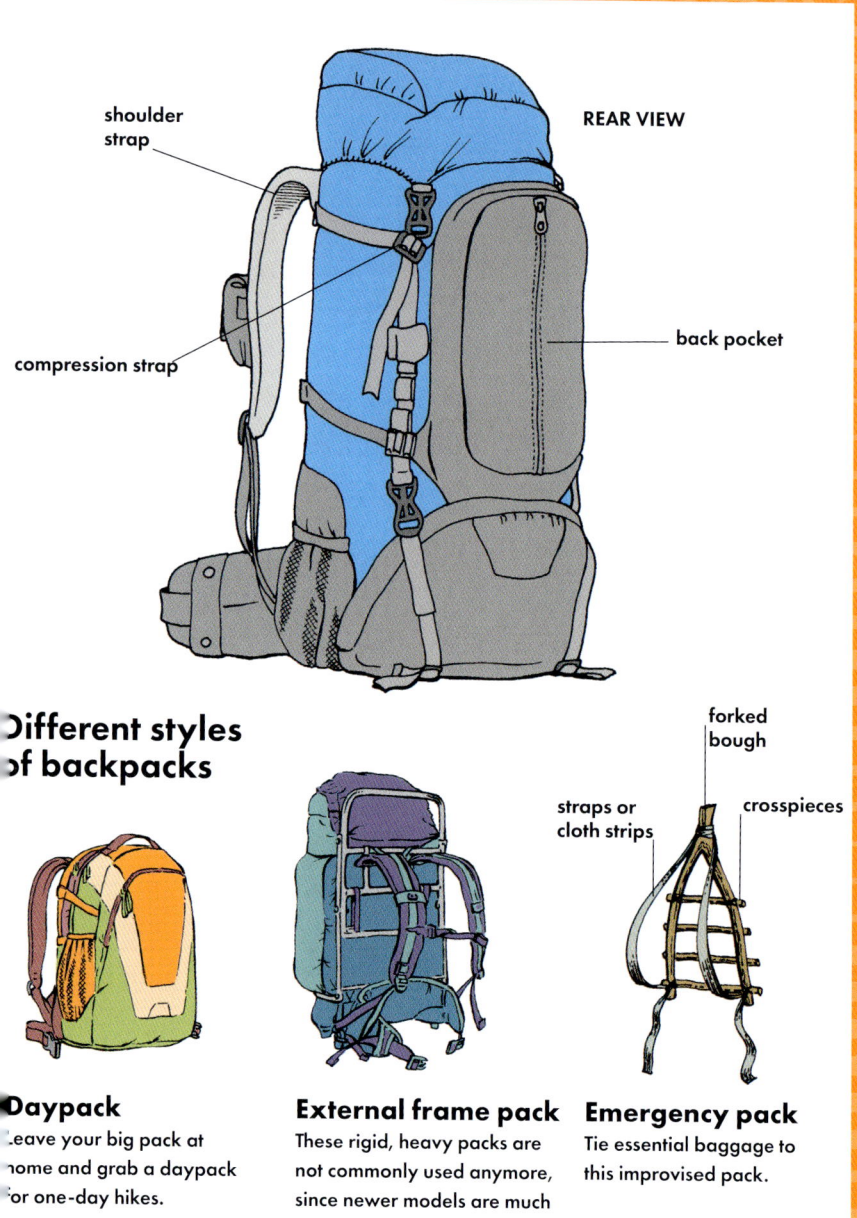

REAR VIEW

shoulder strap

compression strap

back pocket

Different styles of backpacks

forked bough

straps or cloth strips

crosspieces

Daypack
Leave your big pack at home and grab a daypack for one-day hikes.

External frame pack
These rigid, heavy packs are not commonly used anymore, since newer models are much more comfortable.

Emergency pack
Tie essential baggage to this improvised pack.

Make a horseshoe-type pack

This is an emergency backpack that you could make if your backpack gets lost or damaged. It tends to flop into a horseshoe shape when it is picked up.

1 Spread a poncho, tarp, or blanket on the ground.

2 Gather your essential items at one end.

3 Take one edge near the items and roll it over them. Continue rolling to the other end.

4 Tie each end with rope or a similar material.

5 Add extra ties to keep the bundle together, and a line to go over your shoulder and chest.

6 You are ready to face the next challenge!

Pack loading

Even a perfectly fitted, top-of-the-range backpack will be uncomfortable if it is not packed properly. Follow a few simple rules and you will reap the benefits on your journey.

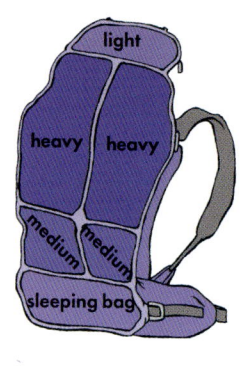

light

heavy heavy

medium medium

sleeping bag

Side view

Put your heaviest gear against your back, near the shoulders.

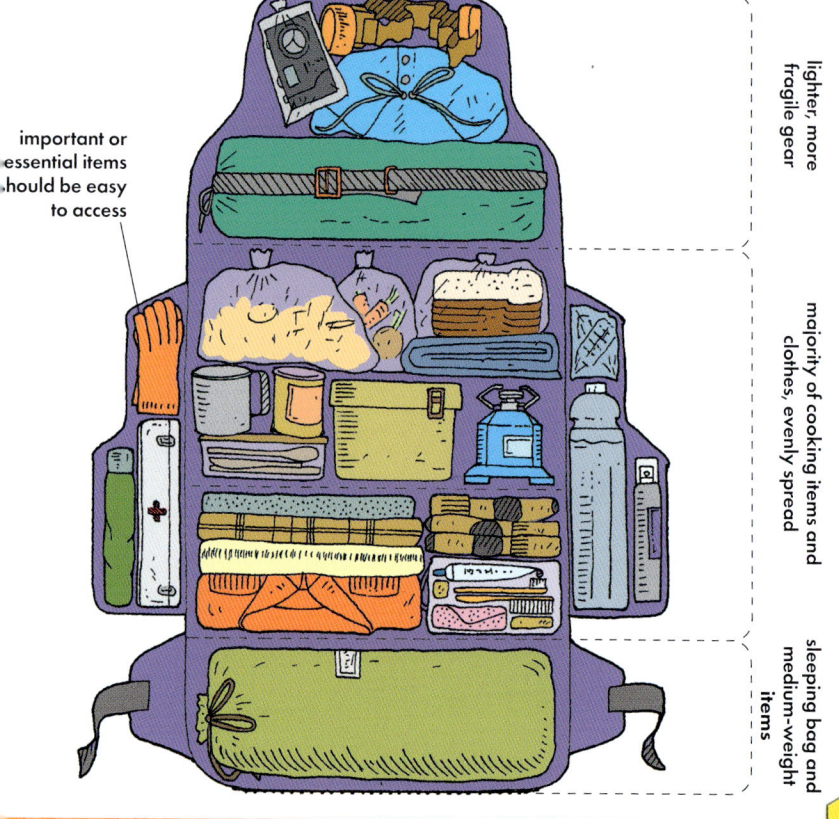

important or essential items should be easy to access

lighter, more fragile gear

majority of cooking items and clothes, evenly spread

sleeping bag and medium-weight items

Straps and buckles

There are many different types of straps and buckles. Make sure you know how they all work on your equipment and that you can rethread them if they come undone. It might be worth taking some spares if you are going for a long hike or the conditions are extreme.

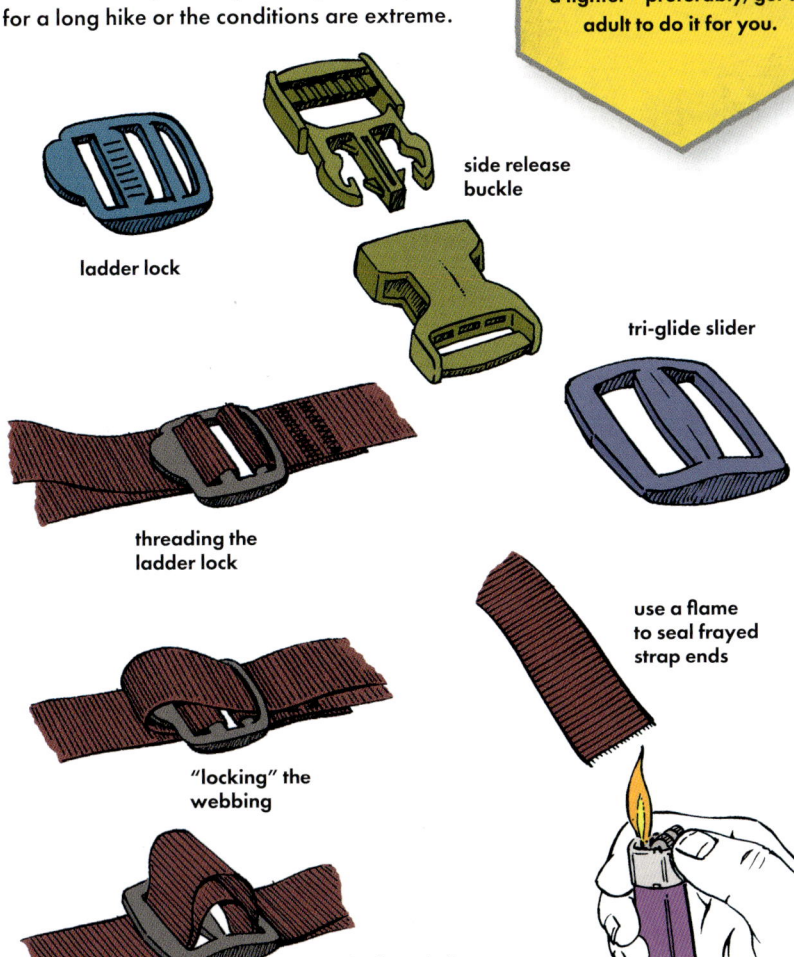

side release buckle

ladder lock

tri-glide slider

threading the ladder lock

use a flame to seal frayed strap ends

"locking" the webbing

properly threaded tri-glide slider

How to put on a pack

Make sure you can lift the backpack safely and it isn't too heavy for you. Sometimes it can be easier if someone else helps you put the backpack on.

1 Keeping your back straight, bend your knee and lift the pack onto it.

2 Bend low. Swivel your body and poke your arm through the shoulder strap.

3 Put your other arm through the shoulder strap on the other side.

4 Fasten the waist harness and adjust the shoulder straps if required.

What to pack

You will need different equipment depending on what sort of hiking you are undertaking. Think about how long you will be out, the possible weather conditions, and the sort of terrain you will come across.

camping stove

food

lighter

first aid kit

water bottle

mobile phone

eating utensils

cup

camera in plastic bag

cooking pot

toiletries

sunscreen

headlamp with spare batteries

maps and compass

waterproof jacket

insect repellent

BEAR SAYS

You will get better at packing as you gain experience. It might be worth making a list of things you wish you'd taken on a hike so you are better prepared in the future.

gloves

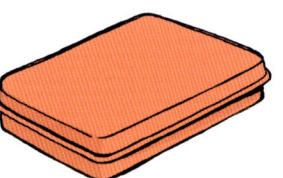
survival kit (see page 12)

clothes

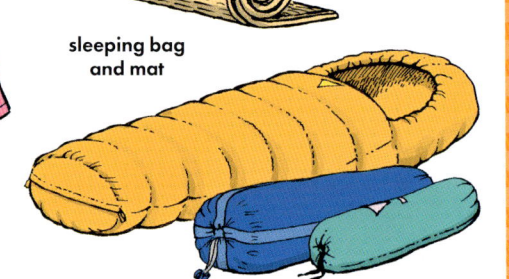
sleeping bag and mat

Survival kit

In a survival situation, a few simple items can mean the difference between life and death. Pack a survival kit according to your needs, and keep it with you whenever you are in the wilderness.

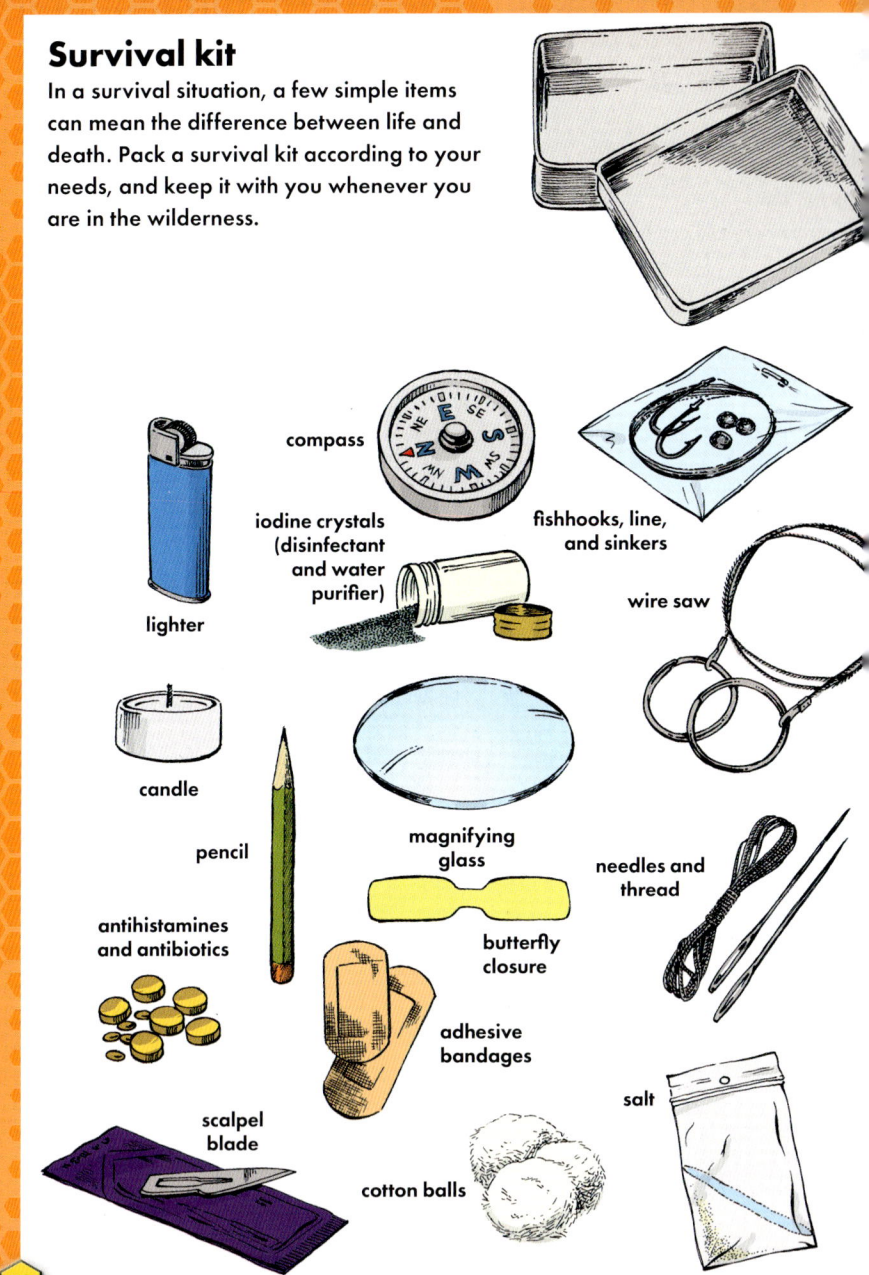

compass

iodine crystals (disinfectant and water purifier)

fishhooks, line, and sinkers

lighter

wire saw

candle

pencil

magnifying glass

needles and thread

antihistamines and antibiotics

butterfly closure

adhesive bandages

salt

scalpel blade

cotton balls

BOOTS

Choose your boots carefully. They must be comfortable and appropriate for your planned activities. Always break in new boots *before* a long hike.

Hiking boot anatomy

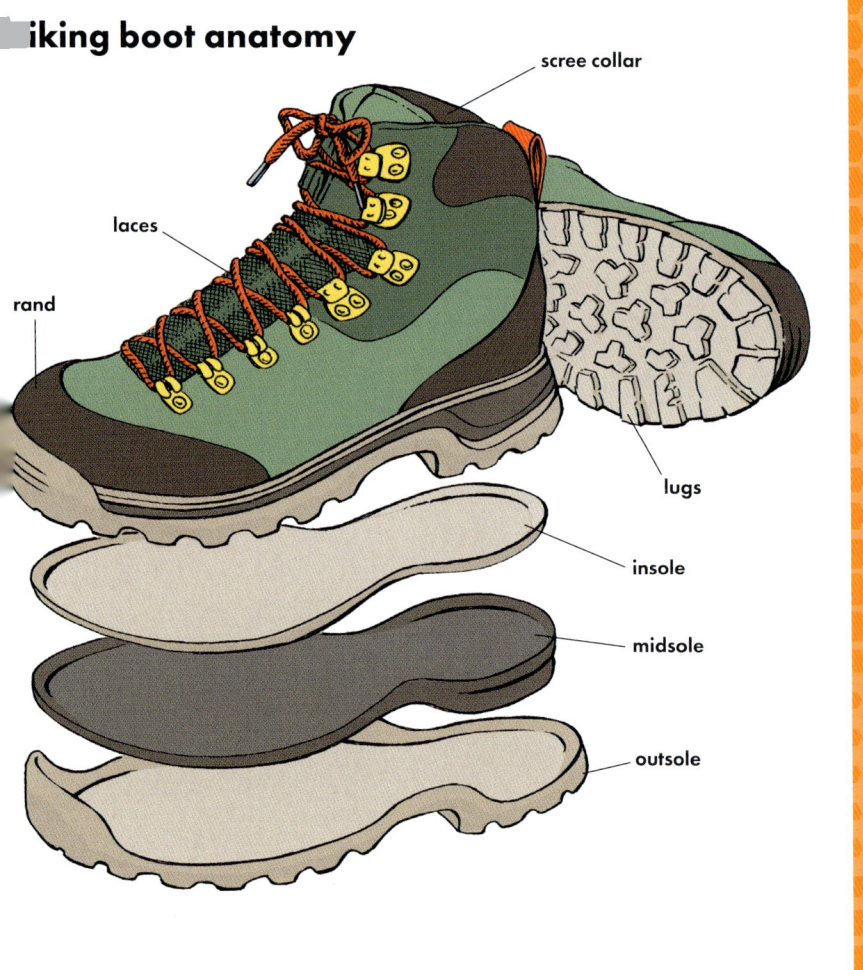

scree collar

laces

rand

lugs

insole

midsole

outsole

Types of boots

It is very important to make sure you have the right footwear. You might be on your feet for a long time, so any discomfort could mean that a pleasant day out becomes miserable toward the end of the hike when you are tired.

Sneaker
These light shoes are sufficient for gentle terrain and won't tear up the earth.

Mountaineering boot
These stiff, insulated boots are not good for regular hiking.

Jungle boot
These canvas and rubber boots are designed to quickly drain moisture.

Desert boot
Suede desert boots allow the feet to breathe, while keeping hot sand out.

Lacing styles and anchors

There are many different ways to lace up your footwear, and several different types of anchors (the part the laces thread through or wrap around). You will need to experiment to find what is comfortable for you and your feet. Some styles don't feel any different, they just look cool!

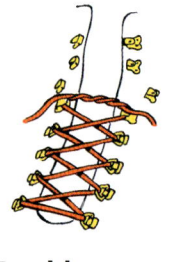

BEAR SAYS

You may want to use skip lacing to avoid footwear rubbing against a foot injury.

Lacing styles

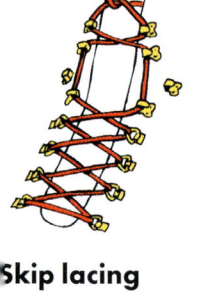

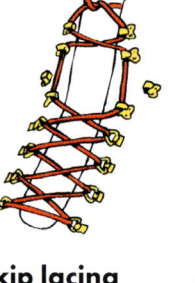

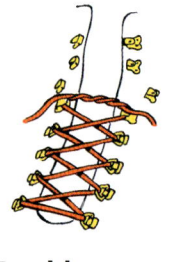

Skip lacing

If you have an injury, or just a high midfoot, skip some anchors when lacing for comfort.

Mountaineer's lace

This simple lacing technique is friction based and won't slip loose.

Double hitch

Tying two separate hitching knots will help relieve pressure and prevent blisters.

Double wrap

Wrap your final knot twice to make it extra sturdy and stop the laces from coming loose.

Lacing anchors

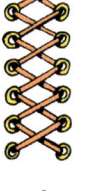

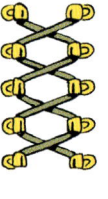

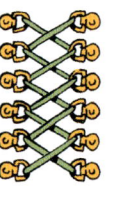

Eyelets   **Webbing**   **Hooks**   **D rings**   **Combination**

Boots through history

Shoes are essential to be able to move safely and comfortably over rough surfaces. The oldest surviving shoes were rope sandals found in Oregon, and are thought to be around 10,000 years old. Boots protect the ankle and sometimes the legs, as well as the feet.

Viking leather boot, ca. 900

medieval greave and sabaton, ca. 1400

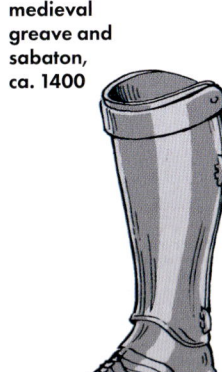

Hessian boot, ca. 1820

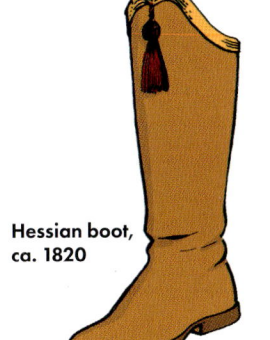

Ötzi the Iceman's boot, ca. 3255 BCE

Inuit sealskin boot, ca. 10,000 BCE—today

Boot care

Hiking boots will last a lot longer and stay in good shape if you take care of them. Always carry spare laces and check for loose stitching or damage each time you wear them.

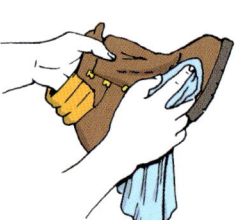

Wash
After a hike, begin by washing the mud and dirt off with water and a soft brush.

Dry
Allow the boots to dry, but keep them away from direct heat from the sun or a fire.

Treat
When the boots are dry, apply a waterproofing or leather nourishing compound.

Socks

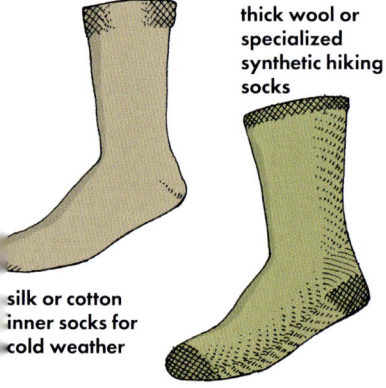

thick wool or specialized synthetic hiking socks

silk or cotton inner socks for cold weather

Trekking poles

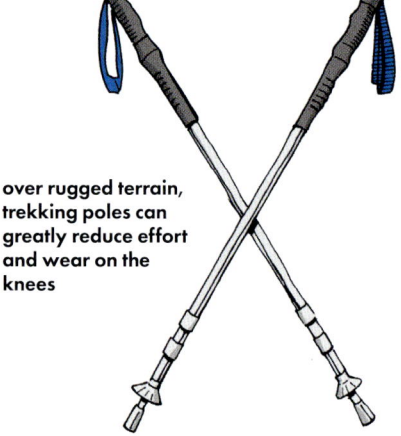

over rugged terrain, trekking poles can greatly reduce effort and wear on the knees

Blister care

Most blisters don't need medical attention and will heal naturally if you leave them alone. Your body will reabsorb any fluid and, as new skin grows, the top layer will become dry and peel off.

1 Leave the blister alone, since letting the fluid out could slow down the healing process and lead to infection.

2 You may choose to cover the blister with a suitable adhesive bandage or dressing. Change the dressing daily and make sure you wash your hands before doing so.

3 Avoid wearing the footwear that caused the blister until it has healed, if at all possible. If a blister has burst, wash it gently and cover it with a dry, sterile dressing.

4 If your blister is extremely painful, red and hot, or filled with pus, it may be infected and you should seek medical advice.

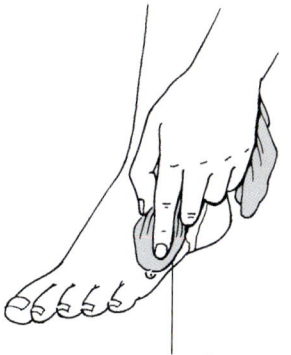

make sure to keep blisters clean to avoid infection

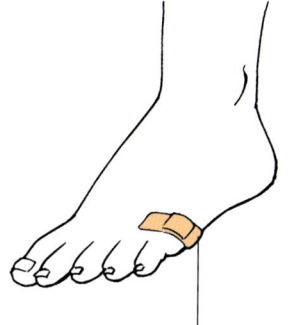

an adhesive bandage can help protect the blister

BEAR SAYS

Always tell an adult about any medical situation, including blisters, so they can decide what to do next.

TRAILBLAZING

Keep an eye out for trail blazes and you won't take a wrong turn. Blazes are markings that lead on from each other to mark the direction of a trail.

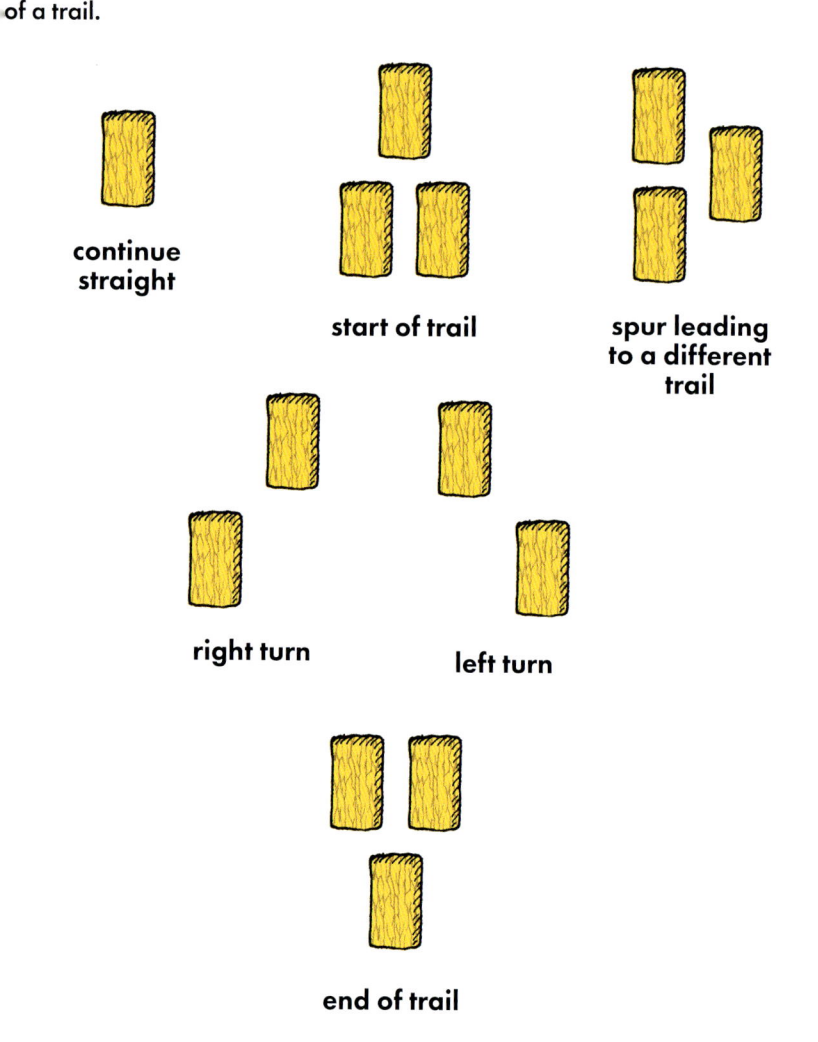

continue
straight

start of trail

spur leading
to a different
trail

right turn

left turn

end of trail

Native American signs

For centuries, the native peoples of North America have left markers for their companions to follow.

continue straight

turn right

turn left

important warning

continue straight

turn right

turn left

important warning

continue straight

turn right

turn left

important warning

JUNGLE TRAVEL

Jungle travel can be tough. Heat, oppressive humidity, biting insects, and thick vegetation will quickly defeat the will of the unprepared.

Jungle strata

emergent layer

canopy layer

understory layer

immature layer

herb layer

Dressing for the jungle

Jungle clothing should be lightweight, strong, and fast drying. Keep a set of clean and dry clothes for sleeping in.

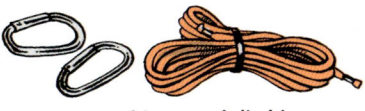

carabiners and climbing rope

wide-brimmed hat

mosquito net

machete

breathable long-sleeved shirt

mosquito coil

water bottle

communication whistle

map in protective case

loose, lightweight trousers

jungle boots

poncho

DESERT TRAVEL

A desert will form anywhere that regularly receives less than ten inches of rain a year. They are places of extreme climates, often very hot by day and extremely cold at night.

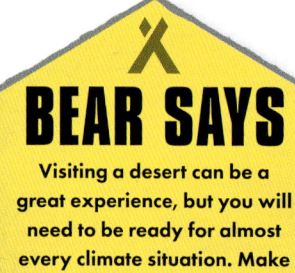

BEAR SAYS

Visiting a desert can be a great experience, but you will need to be ready for almost every climate situation. Make sure you travel with a guide.

Sandy desert
Also known as dune deserts or ergs, sandy deserts are extensive, relatively flat areas covered with windswept sand.

Rocky desert

In some desert regions, the action of wind or intermittent water removes sand and other fine particles, leaving a landscape of bare boulders and pavements of smaller rocks.

Mountain desert

These deserts are made up of barren hills or mountains, often separated by flat basins. Mountain deserts high above sea level can be extremely cold.

Dressing for the desert

Desert clothing must protect the body from the heat of the sun and regulate excessive perspiration. Layers of light-colored clothing made from breathable fabrics are best.

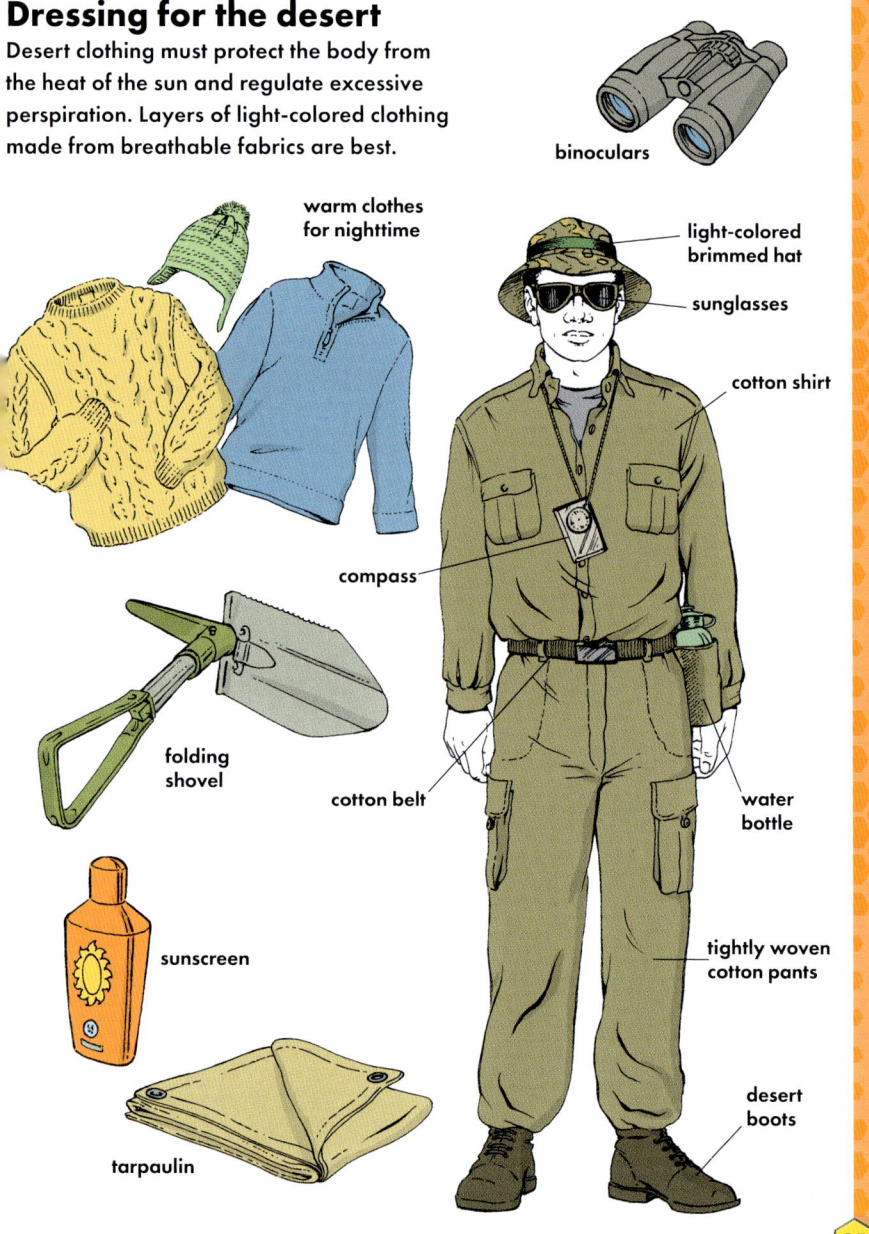

binoculars

warm clothes for nighttime

light-colored brimmed hat

sunglasses

cotton shirt

compass

folding shovel

cotton belt

water bottle

sunscreen

tightly woven cotton pants

tarpaulin

desert boots

Sources of heat

Heat and the body

Desert heat can be a killer. To prevent problems, avoid strenuous exercise, stay hydrated, keep salt levels up, and protect yourself from all sources of heat.

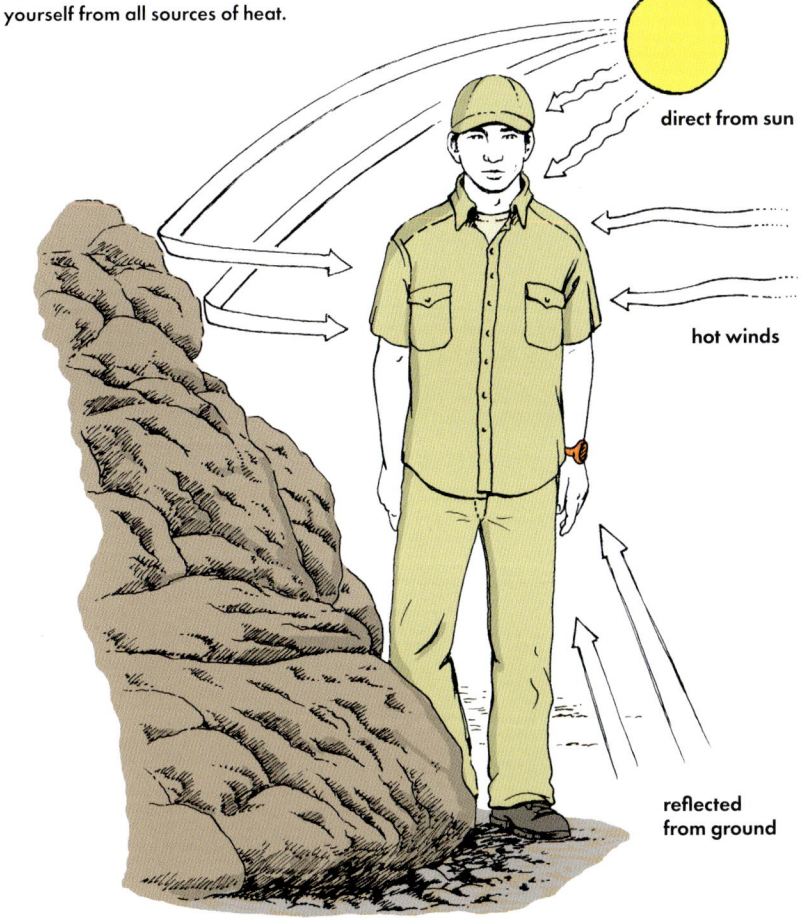

radiant heat from sand and rocks

direct from sun

hot winds

reflected from ground

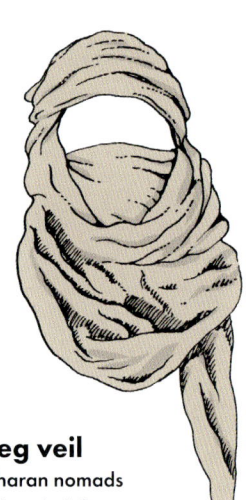

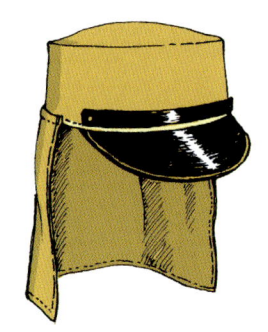

Desert headwear

A hat can make a huge difference to you in the desert. It can literally be the difference between life and death! It protects your hair, eyes, and skin from harmful ultraviolet rays. A good pair of sunglasses would also be useful, in addition to headgear.

French kepi
The space above the head creates an insulating pocket of air.

Tuareg veil
The Saharan nomads favor blue cloth for sun and sand protection.

Cap and cloth
A cap and cloth is an effective, improvised solution.

Safari hat
The safari hat has a wide brim and is permeable to air.

Dunes

Desert dunes are created by windblown sand.
The shape of a dune is influenced by the prevailing
wind direction and the amount of sand available.

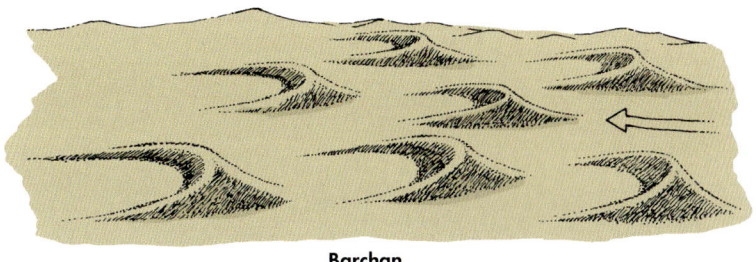

Barchan

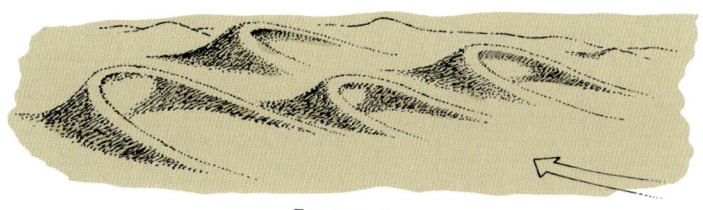

Transverse

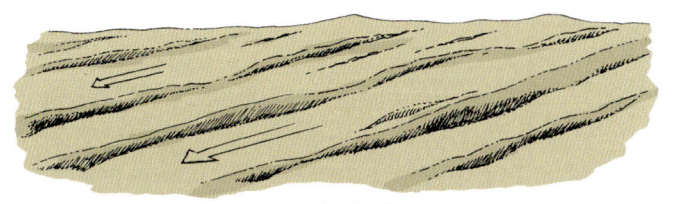

Longitudinal

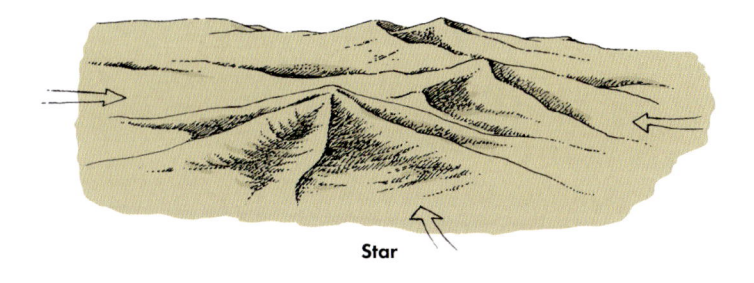

Star

WINTER TRAVEL

Freezing conditions don't mean you have to stay indoors. With the right clothing and equipment, even the most frigid landscapes can be your winter wonderland.

Outdoor winter clothing

ski goggles

wool or synthetic cap or balaclava

insulated windproof jacket over layers of clothing

Dressing for the cold

Wear several layers of clothing in freezing weather—warm air trapped between the layers will insulate you. The outermost layer should be both water- and windproof.

mittens over gloves

windproof insulated pants

thick-soled boots over two pairs of socks

BEAR SAYS

In extreme cold, blood flow to your hands and feet slows down in order to send more blood to your vital organs.

Heat loss

If you get too cold, a hike can become uncomfortable. In extreme cases a condition called hypothermia could develop. The symptoms can vary depending on how low your body temperature has become. If you suspect someone has hypothermia, they need immediate medical attention as soon as possible because extreme cases can be fatal.

Cold and the body

To maintain a healthy body temperature in cold conditions, you must guard against heat loss from several sources.

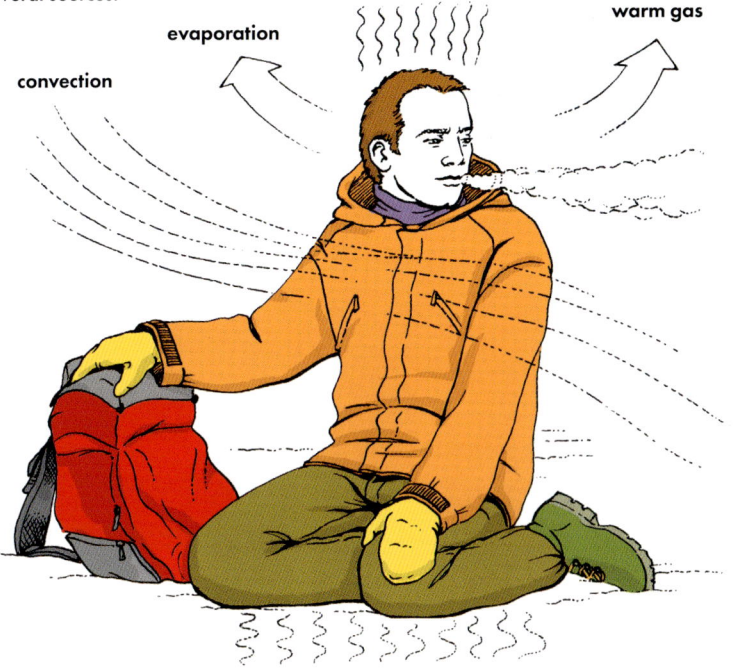

radiation

breathing out moist and warm gas

evaporation

convection

conduction

Wet-weather fabrics

To stay warm, you must stay dry. The original waterproof fabric is oilskin: cotton impregnated with linseed oil. Polyurethane (PU) coated fabric is a cheaper and lighter synthetic alternative. Gore-Tex is a breathable fabric. It keeps water out while allowing perspiration to escape.

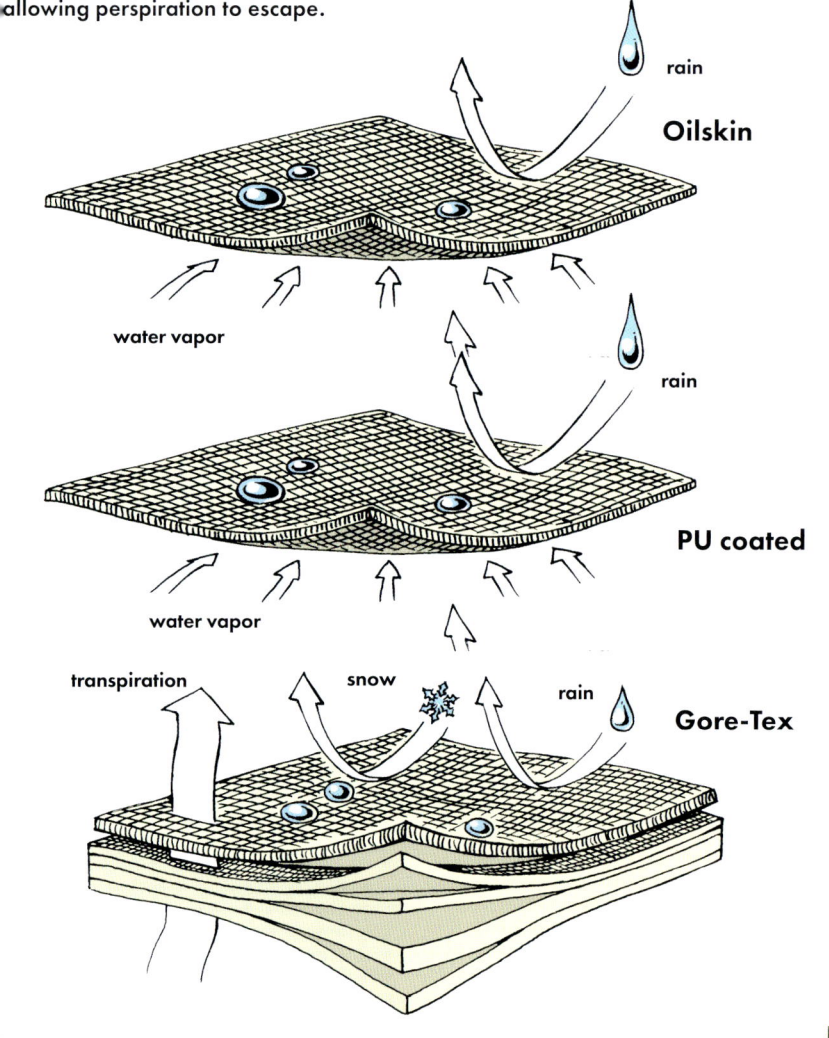

rain

Oilskin

water vapor

rain

PU coated

water vapor

transpiration   snow   rain

Gore-Tex

Cold weather gear

In cold conditions, it's a good idea to pack a range of items that can be removed when exertion is greatest, and then worn as needed, to stay warm when stopping to rest or when the trail is easy.

scarf

balaclava

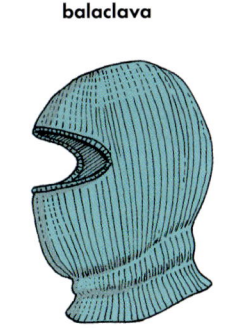

wool beanie

waterproof overmitts with elastic wrist loops

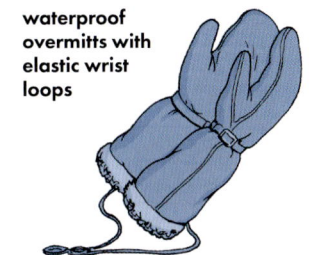

synthetic beanie

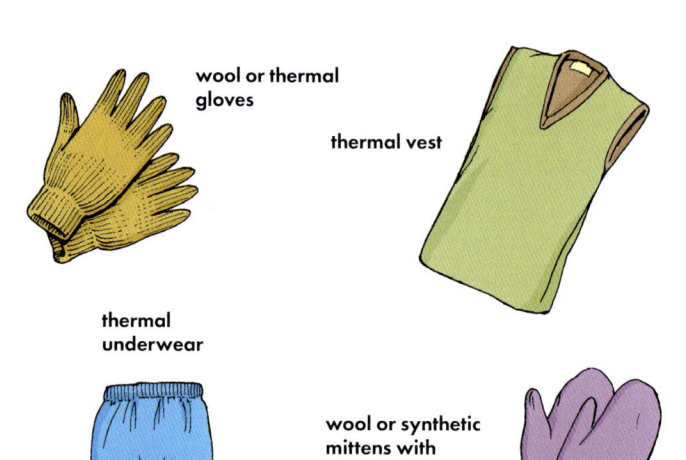

wool or thermal gloves

thermal vest

thermal underwear

wool or synthetic mittens with elastic wrist loops

Snow shoes

If you spread the weight of your body over a larger area, you press down with less force per unit area (lower pressure). This means that you are less likely to sink in snow if you wear wide and long snow shoes rather than normal boots alone.

GLACIER HIKING

Glaciers are rivers of frozen ice found in the polar regions and many mountain ranges. It's always best to walk around them, unless you are part of an experienced team.

Parts of a glacier

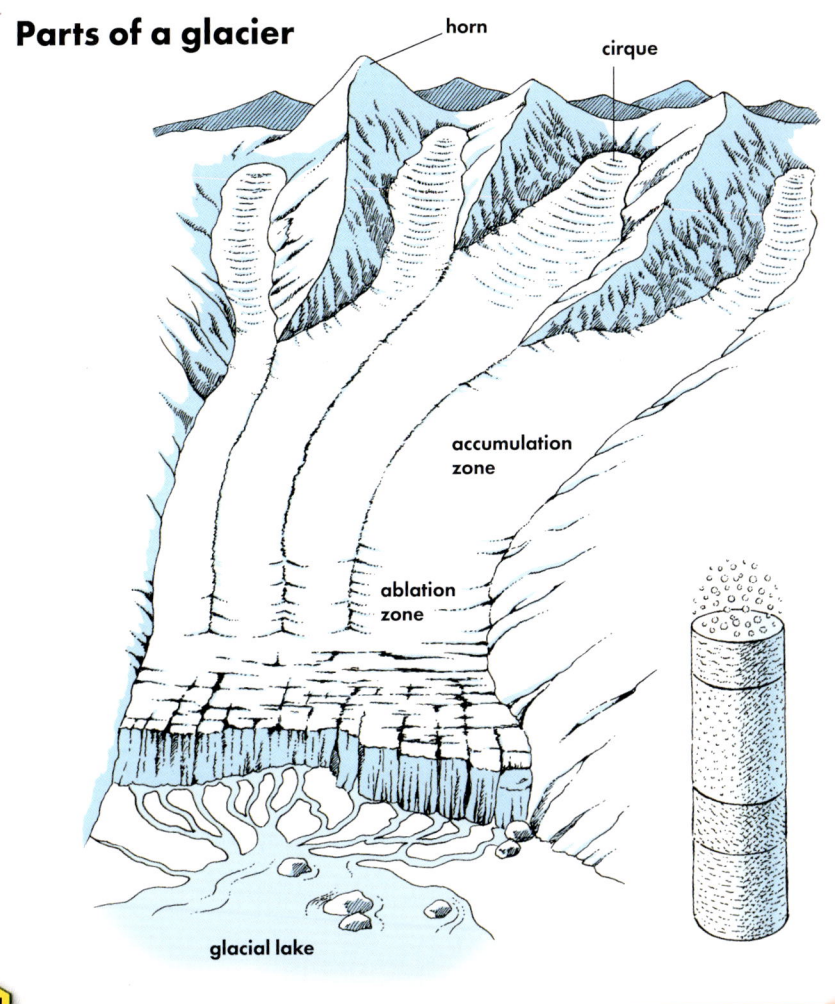

horn

cirque

accumulation zone

ablation zone

glacial lake

How glaciers form

The weight of fresh snow at the top presses the snow beneath it, causing it to become ice.

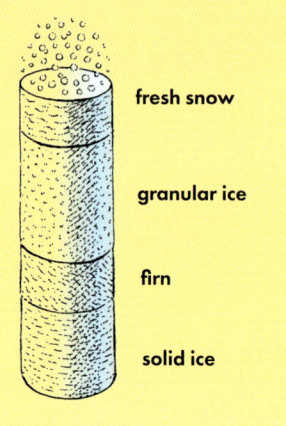

fresh snow

granular ice

firn

solid ice

BEAR SAYS

Always make sure you have the right clothing and equipment for the conditions. If necessary, cancel or delay the hike rather than travel unprepared.

Crevasse

A crevasse is a deep, nearly vertical crack that develops in the upper portion of glacier ice.

crevasses begin to form where the slope on which a glacier flows is irregular—this places stress on the ice, causing cracks to appear

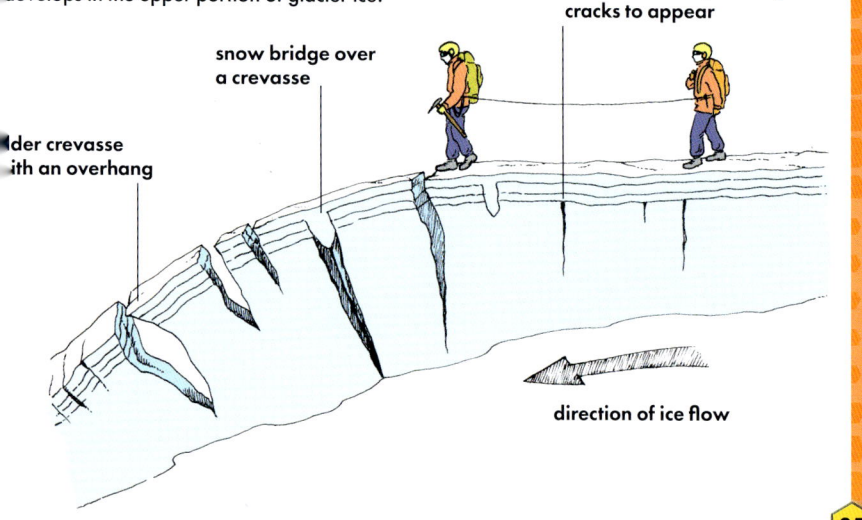

snow bridge over a crevasse

older crevasse with an overhang

direction of ice flow

the lead member of the team checks the thickness of the snow with a pole

Roping up

The first rule of safe glacier travel is to rope up. A rope team of at least three members is recommended, and it's best to have at least two separate rope teams so that a team involved in an accident will have backup help.

Crossing crevasse fields

Crossing a snow bridge

A snow bridge should be examined carefully before the leader attempts a crossing. Other members of the team should be prepared to arrest the leader's fall if the bridge collapses.

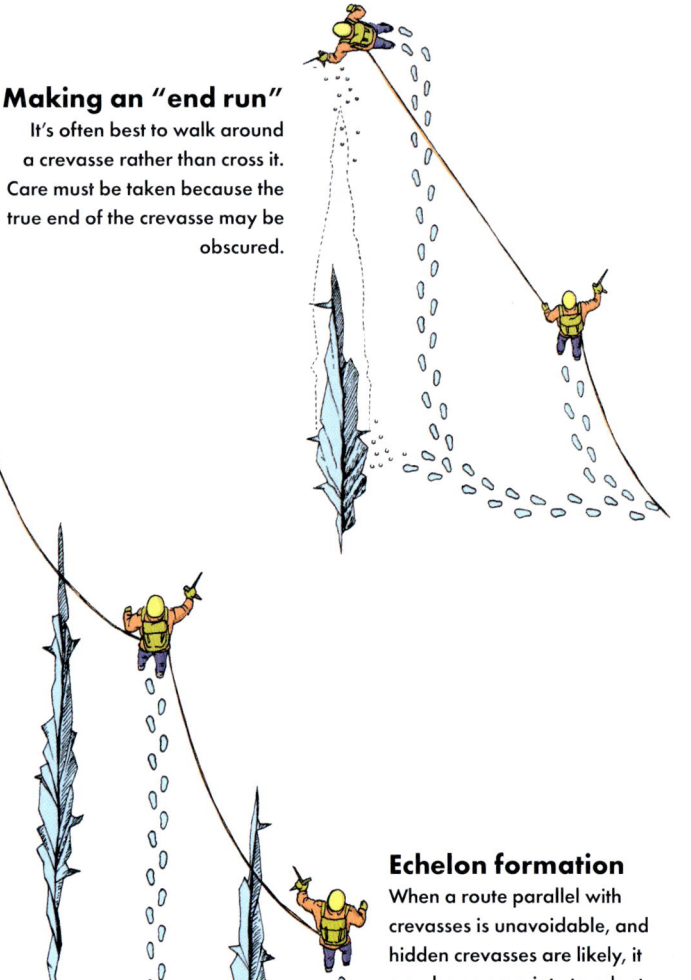

Making an "end run"

It's often best to walk around a crevasse rather than cross it. Care must be taken because the true end of the crevasse may be obscured.

Echelon formation

When a route parallel with crevasses is unavoidable, and hidden crevasses are likely, it may be appropriate to adopt this diagonal formation.

Crevasse rescue kit

This kit is essential for glacier travel. It keeps everything required for a crevasse rescue in one place.

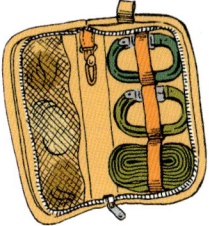

1 When one member of a rope team falls into a crevasse, the other members of the team must immediately move into the self-arrest position. This will stop the victim from falling any deeper into the crevasse.

2 If the fallen hiker is unable to climb up the rope, it is up to the other members of the rope team to effect a rescue. The rescuer closest to the victim releases self-arrest, and sets up a secure anchor in the snow.

3 Once the anchor is secured, all members of the rope team outside the crevasse can work to haul the victim out. Unless the rope party is a large one, a pulley system will need to be set up.

pick or ice axe to stop the rope from cutting into the crevasse lip

HILL WALKING

Hill walking is a great way to get fit, and many areas of incredible natural beauty happen to be hilly. Do it right and you'll have the stamina to cope with the ups and downs all day.

Walking uphill

Small steps
Take shorter steps than usual when heading uphill. Look several footsteps ahead to choose the best route.

Zigzag
For steep ascents, consider taking a zigzag course that will lengthen your route but reduce the gradient.

Hands on
Get your hands dirty by using surrounding rocks and boulders to help you stay balanced and secure on steep ascents.

Walking downhill

Kick your heels in
When walking downhill, take it slowly, keep your back straight, and make sure to put your weight down through your heel on each step.

Trekking poles
Walking downhill can be tough on the legs and knees—trekking poles will help.

Easy descent
Take a zigzag course down a steep slope. It will help you maintain a steady pace.

CROSSING RIVERS

A river without a bridge can be a formidable barrier. While there are many ways to get to the other side, remember that rivers and streams are always dangerous, so approach them with care.

Go with the flow

Trying to swim directly across a river will needlessly waste energy. Swim at an angle to the current.

Wade

Face the current when wading a river. Carry a stout pole to probe your advance and give you extra stability.

Huddle crossing

Three people with linked arms creates a very stable formation when wading. One person should move at a time while the others stabilize him.

direction of flow

direction of travel

direction of flow

Pole assisted

A long, stout pole will provide security for a wading group.

direction of travel

heaviest person on downstream end

Pendulum action

The current at a bend in a fast-flowing river will swing a tethered raft to the far bank.

Ice raft

In cold conditions, rivers may be open in the middle with frozen water by the edges. If the ice is thick enough, cut an ice raft with a saw or axe, and use it to make a crossing.

One-rope bridge

First across

Check that the river is safe for the strongest member of the party to cross. The ideal site will have slow-flowing, shallow water. Once across, the swimmer/wader must securely anchor the end of the rope.

Pulled tight

The remaining members of the party should make a slipknot on the rope and pull the rope taut.

Rappel seat

This is the preferred method. You will need a carabiner and a rappelling harness.

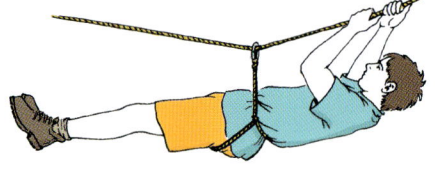

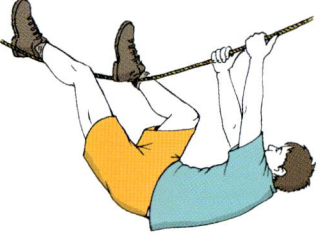

Monkey crawl

Hang below the rope with your hands and both heels crossed over the rope. Pull with your arms, and push your feet to make progress.

Commando crawl

Lie on the rope with your right foot hooked on the rope. Let your left leg hang to maintain balance. Pull with your arms, and push your right foot to make progress.

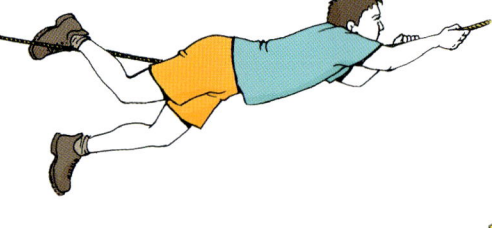

Flotation aids

1 Swing a pair of pants (with ankles tied) through the air at the surface.

2 Thrust the pants into the water, trapping air within.

flotation device

3 You may have to refill the pants with air after a few minutes.

ncho raft

1 Tie the neck of the waterproof poncho and form a ring of plants around the center.

BEAR SAYS

A poncho is basically a waterproof bag with armholes and a hood. It is a light, useful part of your survival equipment in many different situations.

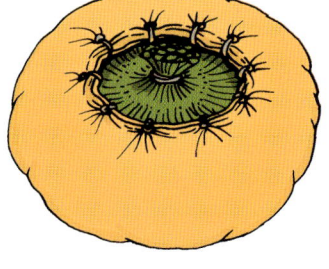

2 Gather up the extremities and tie in a ring around the top center.

Air mattress

Keep your backpack loose so it can be ditched in case you fall in.

More flotation aids

Boards
Four boards secured with rope or nails make a stable raft.

Logs and rope
1 Find two short, dry logs, and tie them together with rope.

2 Seat yourself between the logs and start paddling with your hands.

Make a poncho equipment raft

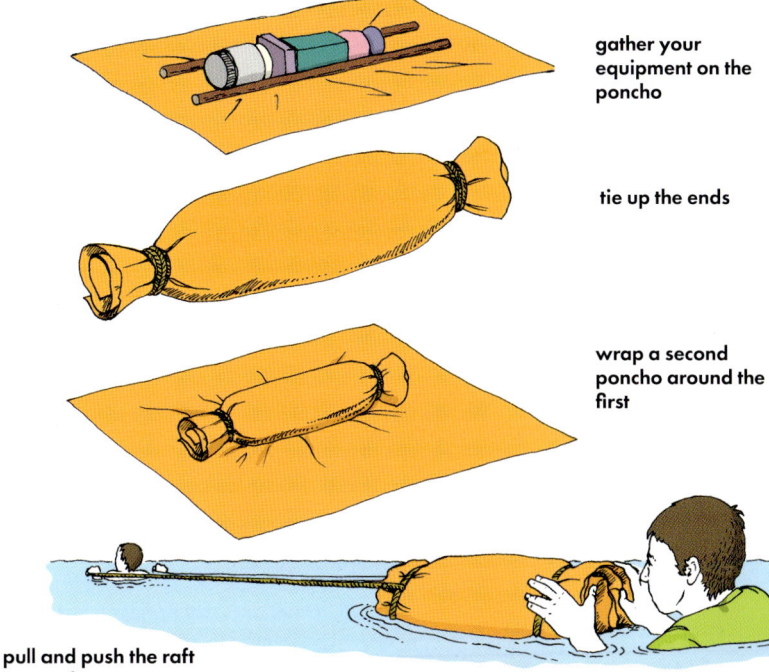

gather your equipment on the poncho

tie up the ends

wrap a second poncho around the first

pull and push the raft across the water

Make a raft

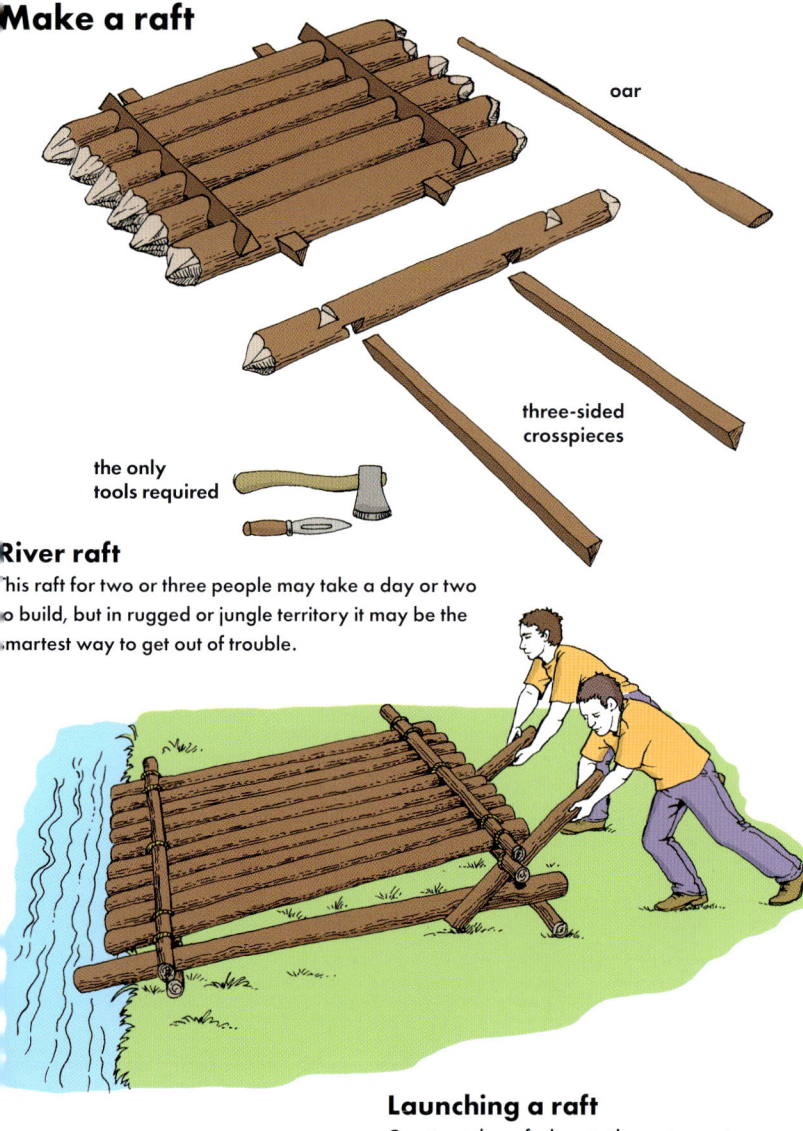

oar

three-sided
crosspieces

the only
tools required

River raft

This raft for two or three people may take a day or two
to build, but in rugged or jungle territory it may be the
smartest way to get out of trouble.

Launching a raft

Construct the raft close to the water on two
smooth logs. Launching the raft is then a simple
matter of levering it up on one side.

Discover all the books in the
Bear Grylls Outdoor Skills Handbook series:

Hiking Adventures

Dangers and Emergencies

Shelter Building

Dangerous Animals

Campfire Cooking

Going Camping

Kane Miller, A Division of EDC Publishing, 2024

Bonnier Books UK in partnership with Bear Grylls Ventures
Produced by Bonnier Books UK
Copyright © 2018 Bonnier Books UK

For information contact:
Kane Miller, A Division of EDC Publishing
5402 S 122nd E Ave
Tulsa, OK 74146

www.kanemiller.com | www.paperpie.com
Library of Congress Control Number: 2023943996

Printed in China
1 2 3 4 5 6 7 8 9 10

ISBN: 978-1-68464-915-0

Disclaimer
Bonnier Books UK, Bear Grylls, and Kane Miller take pride in doing their best to get the facts right in
putting together the information in this book, but occasionally something slips past us. Therefore, we
make no warranties about the accuracy or completeness of the information in the book and to the
maximum extent permitted, we disclaim all liability. Wherever possible, we will endeavor to correct
any errors of fact at reprint.

Kids—if you want to try any of the activities in this book, please ask your parents first! Parents—all outdoor
activities carry some degree of risk and we recommend that anyone participating in these activities be
aware of the risks involved and seek professional instruction and guidance. None of the health/medical
information in this book is intended as a substitute for professional medical advice; always seek the advice
of a qualified practitioner.

MIX
Paper | Supporting
responsible forestry
FSC® C020056

Kane Miller
A DIVISION OF EDC PUBLISHING